C000227994

yo-yo crafts

JODIE DAVIS & JAYNE DAVIS

SELLERS
PUBLISHING

Published by Sellers Publishing, Inc.

Text and photography copyright © 2012 Jodie Davis and Jayne Davis

Sellers Publishing, Inc.
161 John Roberts Road, South Portland, Maine 04106
Visit our Web site: www.sellerspublishing.com
E-mail: rsp@rsvp.com

ISBN 13: 978-1-4162-0698-9
e-ISBN: 978-1-4162-0865-5
Library of Congress Control Number: 2012931576

10 9 8 7 6 5 4 3 2 1

Printed and bound in China.

contents

Introduction & Instruction...4

SNOWFLAKE DOILY 18

POPPY PILLOW...28

ICING DOTS PILLOW 42

YO-YO TRIMMED T-SHIRT 48

MESH BAG A-YO-YO 52

BLOOMING TOTE BAG...56

DOGGIE COLLAR..70

HAIR/SHOE CLIP 74

BEST OF SHOW ROSETTE..78

Patterns..88

About the authors 96

introduction & instruction

How can a simple little circle, gathered into a smaller circle, be so intriguing to so many? Hey, we're talking yo-yos here, so it's no surprise!

Introduced in the 19th century, yo-yos became a fad from the 1920s through the 1940s. Associated with the toy yo-yo, which appeared on the scene at about the same time, yo-yos likewise caught the public's attention. Early quilts were often referred to as "rosette quilts," another fitting name.

Many crafters are familiar with the yo-yo "quilt" made of yo-yos sewn together with no backing. This is more correctly referred to as a coverlet. Many examples also exist of yo-yos sewn to pieces of fabric and then tied rather than quilted.

Making yo-yos is the perfect take-along project, ever available to turn free moments into productive moments. Using a basic stitch, it's a simple process of making long stitches along the edges of circles and then gathering them into smaller circles.

Making Yo-Yos

CIRCLE CUTTING

Before you stitch up your yo-yos, you'll need to cut the circles. The traditional way is to trace around a template. For this, cut a circle out of heavy paper such as a used file folder or piece of cardboard. There are many fabric marking tools on the market. You needn't worry about what you use for marking as long as you cut inside your marked lines. That way the marks are not on your piece. But I like to use Crayola Washable Markers. They really do wash out, but in the meantime you can see the markings.

Cut out your template and trace around it.

Cut out the circle just inside your marked line.

2.

3.

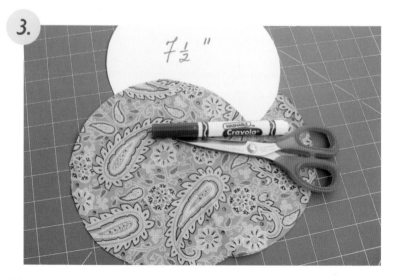

$7\frac{1}{2}$ "

Pucker Up!

Now you're ready to turn those flat circles into fun and funky yo-yos.

Cut a piece of thread 30" or longer. Thread it through a needle, pull the thread through, and knot the two ends together to double it.

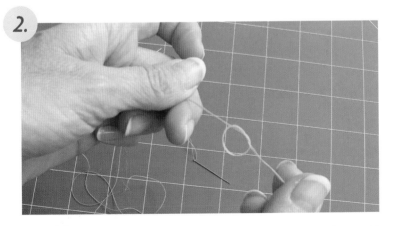

Hold the circle so the wrong side faces you. Starting anywhere on the edge, fold ¼" toward you. NOTE: Icing dollops (see page 42) are an exception. For tiny yo-yos a ⅛" seam allowance is required.

Insert the needle down through both layers and come up through both layers. In this photo Jodie, who is right-handed, is sewing counterclockwise.

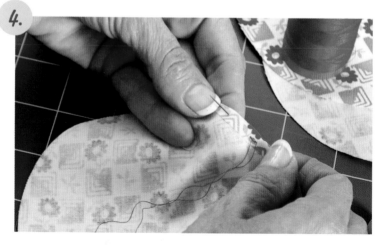

NOTE: The length of your stitches will vary. For the largest yo-yos pictured here, our stitches are an inch long. The icing dollops require stitches of less than ¼".

Continue the running stitch all the way around, finishing where you started (photos 5–8). Do not knot the thread yet.

5.

6.

Pull up on the stitches. Arrange the folds to make them consistent, shaping the yo-yo as you go.

Pull the thread taut.

11.

Make a knot close to your stitching.

12.

You've made a yo-yo!

NOTE: Jayne prefers to stitch her yo-yos from the right side, looking at the front of the yo-yo as she stitches. Jodie works from the wrong side. Neither is right or wrong — do as you please!

13.

Cool Tool Alert: AccuQuilt GO!

Most everyone will agree that cutting the circles to make yo-yos is the most mundane step in the process. It's the old-fashioned route: make a template, mark around it, then cut on the line. Slow.

Fortunately the nice folks at AccuQuilt invented a tool that makes the process fun. The GO! uses dies that turn your scraps or yardage into circles in a snap. It's truly such a thrill that you'll find yourself creating excuses to use the machine! Here's how it works.

First, simply cut your fabric into rough squares. For 5" circles we cut squares about 5½" wide. You can cut multiple circles at a time by layering the squares on the die. We've found that up to four works well. Place them over the 5" circle on the die so their edges go past the circle.

Place the thick plastic piece on top. Now butt the leading edge of the die/fabric sandwich up against the center bar of the Go!

Turning the handle and pushing to help get it started, run the die sandwich through the machine.

After the die has come out the back of the machine, admire your perfect circles!

Of course, when using the GO! you are limited by the dies available. But the AccuQuilt folks are adding more all the time.

COOL TOOL ALERT: CLOVER QUICK YO-YO MAKER

Would you like a little helping hand in getting your yo-yos "just right"? Then this little tool by Clover may do the trick. Two pieces of plastic snap together to encase a roughly cut piece of fabric. Then you trim the edges and sew through the holes in one of the disks. Next pop out your stitched circle.

From here, it's just like the traditional method. Pull up on the threads gently and arrange the pleats as you go, then knot the thread.

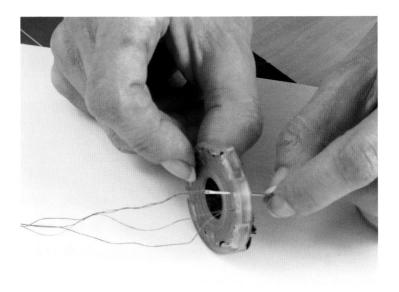

Available just about anywhere, this tool by Clover may tickle your fancy. It comes in a variety of sizes.

SNOWFLAKE DOILY

Finished size: 12" across

Talk about pretty! This little beauty will dress up a table-top, or it can be tacked to the front of a pillow for a striking addition to your sofa. It's even special enough to be framed! We chose tone-on-tone white fabrics to lend a wintery feel. Different color choices will completely change the doily's identity. We found an assortment of beads in our local fabric store. Feel free to vary the sizes for different effects and according to what you have. You may want larger beads when you are using a bolder fabric, for example.

MATERIALS

- ½ yard off-white tone-on-tone fabric
- 1 round ⅜" white pearl bead for large yo-yo center
- 35 light beige ¼" round beads: 11 for edge of center yo-yo and 2 for each bead tail
- 12 brown ⅜" double-cone-shaped beads for small yo-yo centers
- 12 brown ³⁄₁₆" drum beads for bead tails
- 12 white ⅜" teardrop beads for bead tails
- 36 oval-shaped ¼" white pearl beads for bead tails and to connect yo-yos
- 12 tiny (less than ⅛") white pearls to end bead tails
- Matching off-white sewing thread
- Sewing needle
- 12" circle template
- 4" circle template

DIRECTIONS

Cut 1 circle from the fabric using the 12" template. Cut 13 circles using the 4" template. Following the instructions on pages 5–13, make all the circles into yo-yos.

Place the large yo-yo on your work surface. It started out 12" across, and now it should be about 6". This will be the center piece of the doily.

Place a 2" yo-yo over the center of the 6" yo-yo. Sew the ⅜" pearl bead into the center of the yo-yo, stitching through all the layers to bind the bead and yo-yos together.

1.

Sew 11 of the light beige round beads to the outer edge of the center yo-yo, spacing them evenly: String the bead onto your needle, then go down into the edge of the yo-yo and up where the next bead will go. Sew right through the bottom (large) doily as you do so.

2.

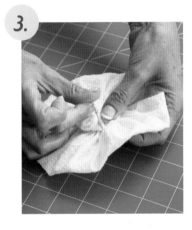

3.

4.

Stitch a ⅜" brown double-cone-shaped bead to the center of another 2" yo-yo. Do not cut the thread.

Push the needle from the middle of the yo-yo, between the layers, and out through one edge.

Arrange the bead tail beads as they will be in the finished tail. (We did the brown drum bead followed by a white teardrop, light beige round, oval pearl, light beige round, and then a tiny white pearl bead.) String them onto your needle. Slide them up on the thread so they are snug to the doily.

7.

8.

9.

Bypassing the bottom bead, run your needle back up through the bead tail.

Pull the thread out above the top bead and knot into the back side of the yo-yo. Cut the thread.

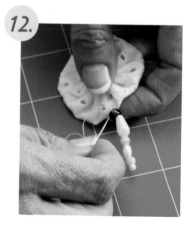

Repeat for all of the small yo-yos.

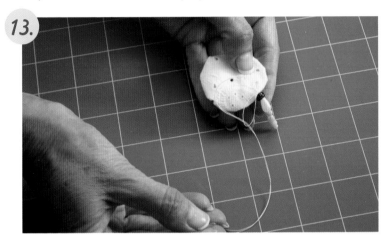

To connect a small yo-yo to the large one, tie a knot in the thread and go into the large yo-yo just under a point along the edge. Pull the thread out and slide an oval-shaped pearl bead onto the needle.

Stitch into the edge of the small yo-yo opposite the tail, then run the needle back up through the bead. Knot and trim the thread.

15.

In the same way, tie a knot in the thread and go into the side of the small attached yo-yo. Pull the thread out, slide an oval pearl bead onto the needle, and stitch into the side of another small yo-yo. Attach the top of this next yo-yo to the large yo-yo.

16.

Continue connecting and attaching small yo-yos, going all the way around the large yo-yo to complete your doily.

17.

18.

POPPY PILLOW

Finished size: 14" x 20"

These perky poppies stand proud atop embroidered stems. The slightly nubbly base of the pillow front fabric sets just the right stage for the poppies. The embroidered chain stitch is quick and easy and provides just the right counterpoint for the puffy blooms. Gold buttons add the crowning touch. Use a heavier complementary fabric for the pillow backing.

MATERIALS

- 14½" x 20½" piece of fabric for front of pillow
- 14½" x 20½" piece of fabric for back of pillow
- 14" x 20" piece of fusible interfacing
- 14" x 20" pillow form
- ½ yard red silky fabric
- ¼ yard dark orange silky fabric
- ¼ yard light orange silky fabric
- ½ yard white silky fabric
- ¼ yard beige silky fabric
- Three ¾" gold buttons
- Chalk or water-soluble fabric marker
- Pearl cotton thread in shades of green
- Embroidery needle
- Sewing thread
- Sewing needle
- Straight pins
- 10" circle template
- 7½" circle template
- 5" circle template

DIRECTIONS

Follow the manufacturer's instructions to fuse the interfacing to the wrong side of the pillow front fabric.

Photocopy the leaf and stem patterns on pages 90–93. Enlarge each page to 140% and tape the four pieces of paper together. See page 94 for overall design reference.

Transfer the design for the stem and leaf embroidery to the right side of the pillow front fabric using chalk or a water-soluble marker. TIP: Taping the pattern to a window with the pillow front fabric on top will enable you to easily see the pattern through the fabric.

2.

Thread your embroidery needle with the green pearl cotton thread. Starting at one end of a stem, embroider over the traced line using consistently sized chain stitches: First, make a knot in the floss. Poke the needle up through the end of the stem from the wrong side of the fabric. Go back into the fabric close to where you came up and pull through from the back, leaving a loop on the top of the fabric. Bring the needle back up through the fabric along the stem line, about ½" from where it went in, and thread it through the loop. Pull up on the thread until the loop lays flat on the fabric, the emerging thread to the inside of the loop. Continue embroidering the stems and leaves, changing shades of green as desired.

3.

4.

5.

6.

7.

Place the pillow front onto the pillow backing fabric with right sides facing. Stitch around the edges with a ¼" seam allowance, leaving an 8" opening at the bottom edge. Trim the seam allowance at the corners. TIP: Stitch the corners at a slight angle.

8.

Turn the pillow cover right side out.

9.

Insert the pillow form into the cover.

10.

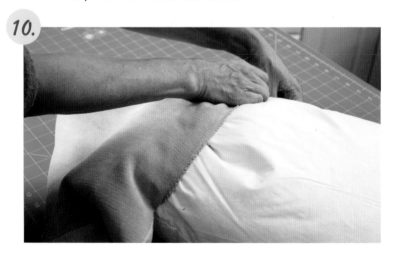

11.

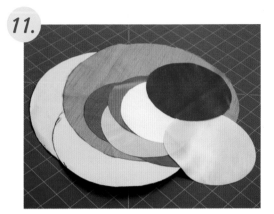

Following the instructions on pages 5–13, make the following yo-yos out of the silky fabrics:

- 1 red yo-yo using the 10" circle template
- 2 dark orange yo-yos using the 10" circle template
- 1 light orange yo-yo using the 10" circle template
- 1 white yo-yo using the 10" circle template
- 1 beige yo-yo using the 10" circle template
- 3 white yo-yos using the $7\frac{1}{2}$" circle template
- 1 red yo-yo using the $7\frac{1}{2}$" circle template
- 2 beige yo-yos using the $7\frac{1}{2}$" circle template
- 2 dark orange yo-yos using the $7\frac{1}{2}$" circle template
- 1 light orange yo-yo using the $7\frac{1}{2}$" circle template
- 1 white yo-yo using the 5" circle template
- 1 red yo-yo using the 5" circle template
- 2 dark orange yo-yos using the 5" circle template
- 1 light orange yo-yo using the 5" circle template
- 2 beige yo-yos using the 5" circle template

Arrange the large and medium yo-yos on the front of the pillow. Hand stitch through the yo-yos into the pillow front fabric to attach them, reaching in through the opening in the bottom of the pillow as needed. Hide the stitches in the folds of the yo-yos.

Place the small yo-yos at the centers of the large yo-yos. Attach them to the pillow fabric, stitching through the large yo-yos.

15.

16.

Stitch the 3 gold buttons to the centers of 3 of the double yo-yo sets.

17.

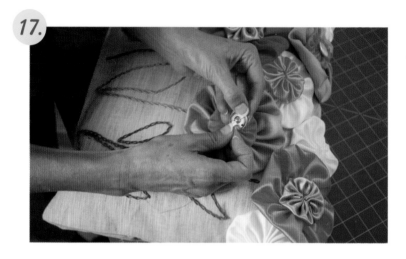

18.

Pin the opening closed, with the straight pins running along the seam. Hand stitch the opening closed.

19.

icing DOTS PiLLOW

Finished size: 16" x 16"

Tiny yo-yo dots, like dollops of icing from a cake-decorating bag, are arranged in delicious arcs on this contemporary-looking pillow. Sewn from tiny fabric circles, the yo-yos pucker somewhat when gathered, giving that icing-like effect.

For our project, we chose a green upholstery fabric akin to a fine-wale corduroy. The yo-yos are tone-on-tone white cotton prints.

MATERIALS

- ³/₄ yard white tone-on-tone fabric for yo-yos
- Two 16¹/₂" x 16¹/₂" squares of fabric for pillow
- 16" x 16" pillow form
- Water-soluble fabric marker
- White sewing thread
- Sewing needle
- Straight pins
- 2" circle template

DIRECTIONS

1. Cut out 46 circles from the white fabric using the 2" template.

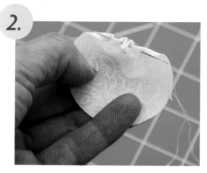

2. Follow the instructions on pages 5–13 to turn them into yo-yos, using a ⅛" seam allowance. NOTE: The yo-yos will be small and will pull up into a pucker, much like a small dollop of icing.

3.

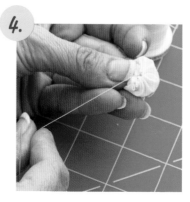

4.

5.

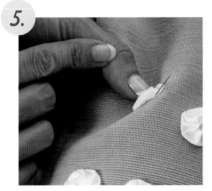

Photocopy the pattern for the layout of the yo-yos on page 95, enlarging to 200%. To transfer the design for the layout of the yo-yos onto the pillow front, tape the pattern to a window. Tape one piece of pillow fabric over the pattern, and using a water-soluble marker, transfer the dots for the placement of the yo-yos.

6.

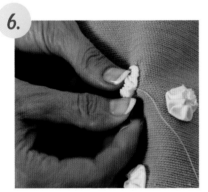

Hand stitch the yo-yos in place, sewing through the centers and backs of the yo-yos to secure them.

7.

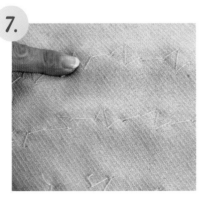

This is how the back will look after you stitch the yo-yos on.

8.

Place the pillow front onto the backing fabric with right sides facing. Align the edges. Stitch around the edges with a ¼" seam allowance, leaving an 8" opening at the bottom edge.

9.

Trim the seam allowance at the corners.

10.

Turn the pillow cover right side out.

Insert the pillow form into the cover.

11.

Pin the opening, then hand stitch closed.

12.

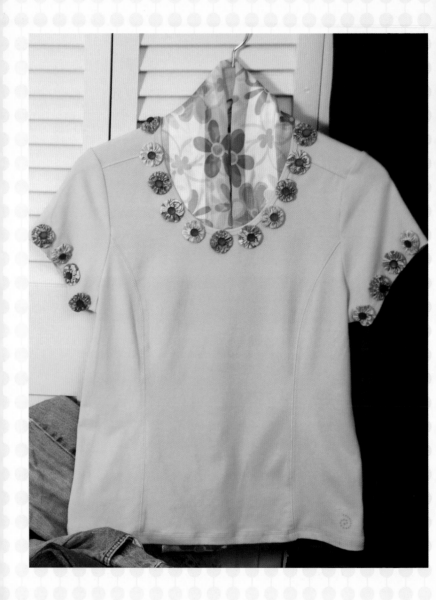

yo-yo trimmed t-shirt

Start with a T-shirt, add some yo-yos and buttons, and suddenly what was plain becomes something special! We chose a nicely shaped T-shirt for our blank canvas. The fabric is stretchy cotton, and the princess seaming is flattering. The yo-yo fabric is a cotton from one of Jodie's local quilt shops, Tiny Stitches in Marietta, Georgia. Jayne used the 3" AccuQuilt GO! die to cut the circles for the yo-yo. She's rather addicted to the thing. Come to think of it, so is Jodie.

MATERIALS

- *T-shirt*
- *½ yard fabric for yo-yos*
- *32 buttons, ⅜" or ½"*
- *Matching sewing thread*
- *Sewing needle*
- *3" circle template*

DIRECTIONS

Cut out 32 circles from the yo-yo fabric using a 3" template. Make 32 yo-yos from the circles following the instructions on pages 5–13.

Arrange 16 of the yo-yos along the neckline of the T-shirt — 9 on the front and 7 on the back: First, pin 1 at the center front, and then pin 1 at each shoulder seam. On the front, space the remaining 6 yo-yos evenly, 3 on one side and 3 on the other, and pin.

Distribute the remaining 7 yo-yos across the back neck edge and pin.

Arrange 8 yo-yos along the edge of each sleeve, 4 on the back and 4 on the front, and pin in place.

From the inside of the T-shirt, hand stitch through the T-shirt into the back of a yo-yo by making a stitch in the back of the yo-yo about halfway between the center of the yo-yo and the outer edge. Working your way around the yo-yo, take a stitch into the T-shirt, then in the back of the yo-yo.

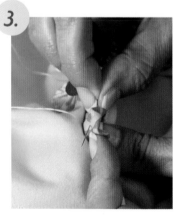

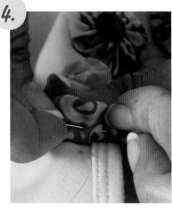

When you get back to the first stitch, bring your needle up through the center of the yo-yo. Use it to add a button to the center of the yo-yo.

Knot the thread and cut it, then move on to the next yo-yo.

MESH Bag a-yo-yo

The simple addition of some bead-adorned yo-yos turns an ordinary cotton shopping bag into something special. We chose large stone beads with holes at the sides. You may have buttons that are "just right" for your bag, and the extra-wide rickrack is widely available these days in all sorts of great colors. Jodie found the mesh bag online. Search for "EuroSac Natural Cotton String Bag." It comes in colors too. Fun!

MATERIALS

- Mesh bag
- Scraps of fabric for yo-yos, about ½ yard
- 10 buttons or beads, ¾" wide
- 2 yards rickrack
- Sewing thread to match rickrack
- Sewing needle
- Straight pins
- 5" circle template

DIRECTIONS

Cut out 10 circles from the scrap fabric using a 5" template. Following the instructions on pages 5–13, make 10 yo-yos.

Starting at the bottom of one handle, at the intersection of the handle and one "underarm" (that's what it looks like!),pin the rickrack along the webbing strap, centering it in the webbing. Hand stitch the rickrack onto the strap.

Fold the bag to find the center back and center front. Hand sew yo-yos to these spots. Sew a yo-yo to each of the intersections where the handles meet the top of the bag. Then add a yo-yo in between each of the yo-yos that are already attached. You will have 5 yo-yos on the front and 5 on the back of the bag.

1.

2.

Sew the buttons or beads to the centers of the yo-yos.

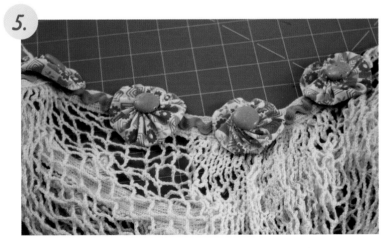

Blooming Tote Bag

Finished size: 11" x 14"

This pretty tote isn't your grocery bag variety. Nope, this one is lovely enough to stand in for a purse. For the body of the tote, Jodie chose a woven fabric from the upholstery section of a local decorator fabric store. It smacks of burlap but is much, much softer and higher in quality. It is the perfect backdrop for the yo-yo flowers and the webbing straps. The lining and binding are made of quilting cotton.

MATERIALS

- *Scraps of 4 coordinating fabrics for flower*
- *17½" x 28½" piece of fabric for tote body*
- *17½" x 28½" piece of lining fabric*
- *Two 2" x 7½" strips of fabric for the binding*
- *Two 17" x 28" sheets of Wonder-Under or other fusible web*
- *Two 52" lengths of 1"-wide webbing*
- *Sewing thread*
- *Sewing needle*
- *Straight pins*
- *7½" circle template*
- *6" circle template*
- *5" circle template*
- *3" circle template*

DIRECTIONS

Remove the paper from one side of a sheet of fusible web.

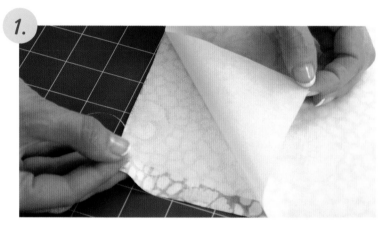

Place the lining fabric right side down. Center the fusible web on top of the lining, sticky side down, and finger press gently in place. Starting at a corner, peel back the paper from the fusible web and remove.

Lay the body fabric, right side up, on top of the fusible web, carefully aligning the edges with the lining below.

Fuse with a hot iron according to the manufacturer's instructions.

Using a zigzag or other finishing stitch, machine stitch along the long edges of the fabric sandwich.

Press the binding strips in half lengthwise, right side out.

5.

Align the raw edges of one of the folded pieces of binding with the raw edge of one of the short sides of the fabric sandwich. Working from the right side of the tote, stitch the binding strip to the tote with a ¼" seam. Repeat with the other strip of binding on the other short side of the fabric sandwich.

6.

Fold the binding strips up and press away from the tote with a hot iron.

7.

The binding strips should extend above what will be the top edges of the tote.

8.

With the right side of the fabric sandwich facing up, measure the halfway point along one of the long edges of the fabric. Measure 4" from that point and mark with a pen. Repeat on the other side of the bag.

9.

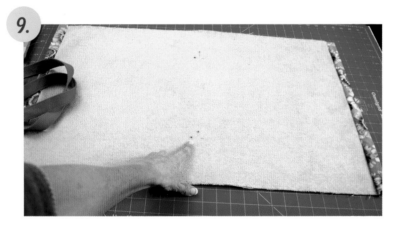

10.

Lay one piece of webbing (for the strap) on the fabric so that one end of the strap butts up against a pin and the other end runs over the binding on one end of the fabric. Bend the strap around until it butts against the other pin. Pin in place.

Stitch close to the edge of the webbing. Starting at the bottom of one end of the strap, sew up one side, across just below the binding, and down the other side. Repeat on the other end of the strap. Repeat this process to attach the other strap.

11.

Fold the fabric in half with the right sides facing and the handles side by side. Stitch the side seams ¼" from the edge.

Press the seams open. (A pressing ham comes in handy for this.)

To make box corners, open a bottom corner and flatten so the side seam runs down the center of the triangle. Draw a line perpendicular to the side seam and 2" from the corner. The line should be about 4" long. Stitch along the line. Repeat on the other side.

15.

16.

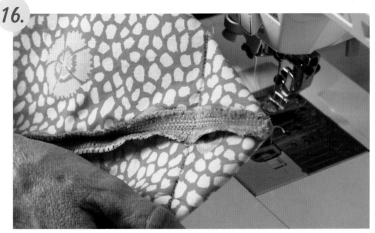

Fold the binding over the raw edges to the inside and press with a hot iron. Hand stitch the binding to the inside of the bag.

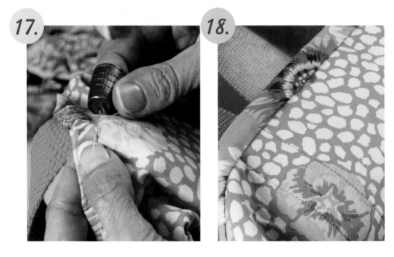

Hand sew the points of the box corners to the bottom of the bag.

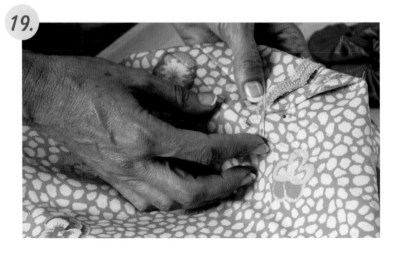

Make 6 yo-yos using the 6" template for the outer flower petals. Make 1 yo-yo using the 7½" template for the backmost center yo-yo. Make 1 yo-yo using the 5" template for the middle center yo-yo. Make 1 yo-yo using the 3" template for the topmost center yo-yo.

20.

Arrange the yo-yos into a flower.

21.

Sew the yo-yo flower together through all the layers.

22.

Place the flower just above the center of the front of the bag and hand stitch into place. Knot the thread inside the bag.

23.

Doggie Collar

Dress up your doggie yo-yo style with this woofy-approved "I'm cute!" collar. (Dad's Pound Puppy "Zoe" loves hers, even if she is shy about the camera.) You'll need more or less elastic and yo-yos depending on the girth of your pooch's neck. This is a perfect project for using up leftover fabric. We used prints for the large yo-yos and a white-on-white fabric for the centers.

MATERIALS

- Scraps of fabric
- 1"-wide elastic
- Sewing thread
- Sewing needle
- 5" circle template
- 2" circle template

DIRECTIONS

Following the instructions on pages 5–13, make enough 5" yo-yos to go around your dog's neck with the edges just touching.

Make the same number of 2" yo-yos using a $\frac{1}{8}$" seam allowance. They will be poufy!

Measure the circumference of your dog's neck and cut a piece of elastic 1" longer. Overlap the ends of the elastic by 1" and sew them together by machine or by hand.

Hand sew the larger yo-yos to the elastic, spacing them so they just touch.

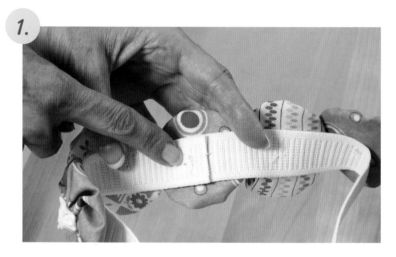

Sew the smaller frosting-dollop yo-yos to the centers of the larger yo-yos.

3.

HAIR/SHOE CLIP

A super-quick project, these little clips can dress up a myriad of otherwise plain items. Don't stop at your hair or shoes; try clipping a yo-yo pair onto the ribbon of gift packages, or use one to hold a note on a magazine or book or to clip a love note to the shade of a lamp. These little clips make it easy to take something from simple to special!

MATERIALS

- Scraps of fabric
- Matching sewing thread
- Beads or buttons
- Hair clip
- Hot glue and glue gun
- 5" circle template
- 4" circle template

DIRECTIONS

Make 1 yo-yo using the 5" template, and make 1 using the 4" template, following the instructions on pages 5–13.

Place the smaller yo-yo on top of the larger yo-yo. Sew the bead or button into the center of the top yo-yo, stitching through all the layers to bind the bead and the yo-yos together into a rosette.

Turn the rosette over and place a dollop of hot glue in the center. Press the top of the hair clip into the glue and hold in place until it cools. Be careful not to glue the clip shut!

3.

4.

5.

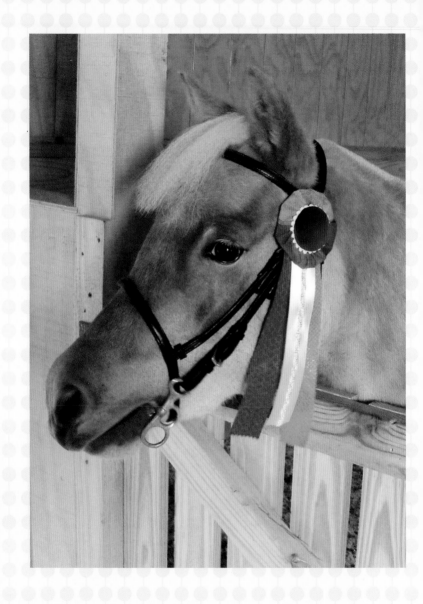

BEST OF SHOW ROSETTE

Create a pretty memento for every winner in your stable or home with this easy, quick, and super-cute project. It's simply one yo-yo, a covered button, and three pieces of ribbon, all hot glued together. Can you hear the whinnies of delight already?

While Tina loves hers, you don't have to have miniature horses to be able to pin your winners. Canines and even humans will lap up the appreciation!

MATERIALS

- *8" square piece of fabric for yo-yo*
- *3" square piece of velvet or other fabric to cover button*
- *1½" coverable button*
- *Three 12"-long pieces of ribbon*
- *12" length of ¼"-wide braid*
- *7" length of trim for rosette*
- *12" length of flat trim (optional)*
- *Hair clip*
- *Hot glue and glue gun*
- *Scraps of card stock (file folders work great)*
- *7½" circle template*
- *3" circle template*

DIRECTIONS

Make the yo-yo using the 7½" template and following the instructions on pages 5–13.

1.

Using the 3" template, cut out a 3" circle from the velvet. Cover the button with the velvet, following the button manufacturer's instructions. First, catch the fabric in the teeth of the button at 9 o'clock and 3 o'clock, then at 12 o'clock and 6 o'clock, and then work in between. (For these big buttons and the thick velvet, Jodie used a small hammer to get the backing in place.)

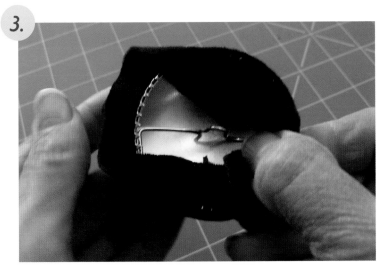

Hot glue the trim to the back edge of the button, cutting off any extra length.

4.

Trim both ends of the ribbons with pinking shears.

5.

Dab hot glue onto an end of one of the pieces of ribbon and lay the end of another ribbon over it at a slight angle, fanning out the "bottom" ends. Add the third ribbon, making sure the glued ends of the ribbon are stacked and the other ends are spread apart slightly in an attractive fan shape.

6.

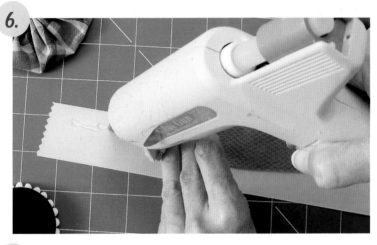

7.

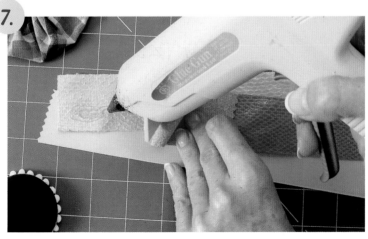

If desired, hot glue a strip of flat trim to the center of the middle ribbon.

8.

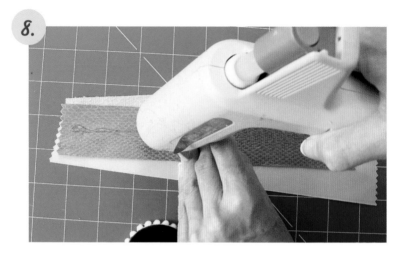

9.

Add hot glue to the back of the covered button and press over the hole in the center of the yo-yo.

Place a large dollop of hot glue at the top end of the ribbons and add the yo-yo rosette. Press down firmly.

Using the 3" template, trace a 3" circle onto the piece of card stock and cut out. In our example, one side of the card is white and the other side is green. Cover one side of the card stock circle with hot glue and attach it, glue side down to the back of the ribbon, covering the ends of the ribbon.

13.

14.

Place a dollop of hot glue in the center of the card stock backing and press the hair clip into the glue (see photo #4 on page 77 for reference). Attach the clip in the direction that works for what you are going to clip it to. For example, if you will be clipping the ribbon to the left side of a horse's bridle as in the photo on page 78, the open end of the hair clip should face left as you look at the cardboard back. TIP: Hold the clip open with a large needle or small screwdriver while it dries.

15.

Patterns

The patterns are drawn to fit the page size. As a result some will need to be enlarged on a photo copier. Beginning on page 90, each pattern piece will state the number to be cut.

YO-YO CIRCLE TEMPLATES

4" Circle Template
(use at 100%)

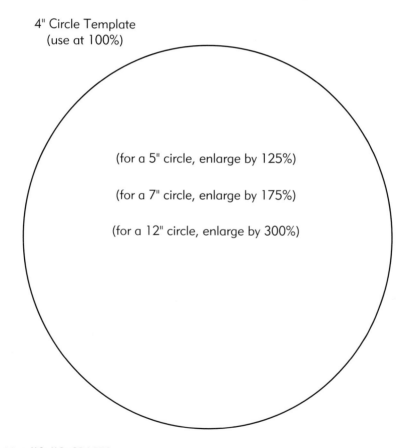

(for a 5" circle, enlarge by 125%)

(for a 7" circle, enlarge by 175%)

(for a 12" circle, enlarge by 300%)

YO-YO CIRCLE TEMPLATES

2" Circle Template
(use at 100%)

3" Circle Template
(use at 100%)

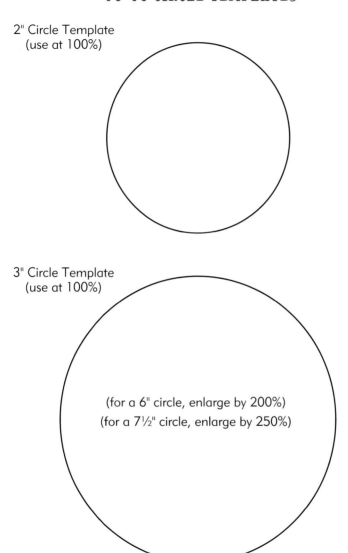

(for a 6" circle, enlarge by 200%)
(for a 7½" circle, enlarge by 250%)

POPPY PILLOW

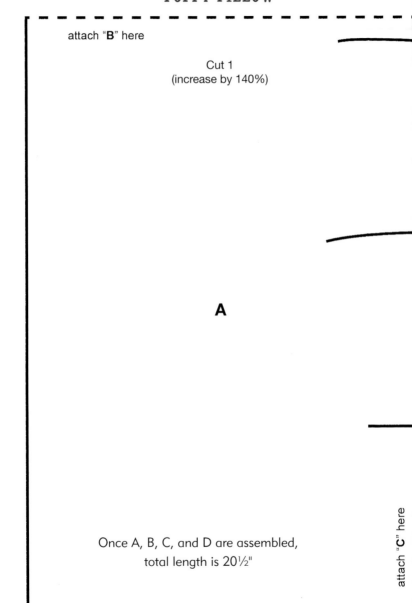

attach "**B**" here

Cut 1
(increase by 140%)

A

attach "**C**" here

Once A, B, C, and D are assembled,
total length is 20½"

POPPY PILLOW

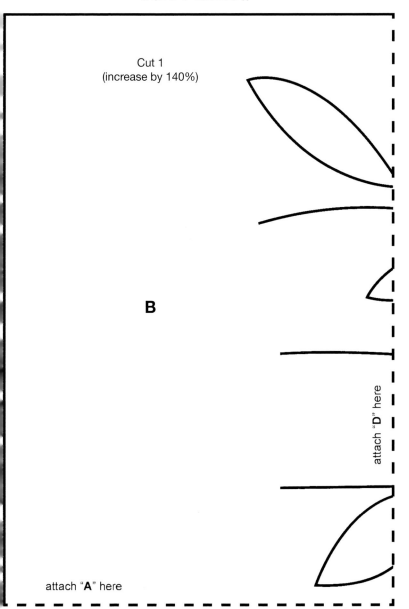

Cut 1
(increase by 140%)

B

attach "**D**" here

attach "**A**" here

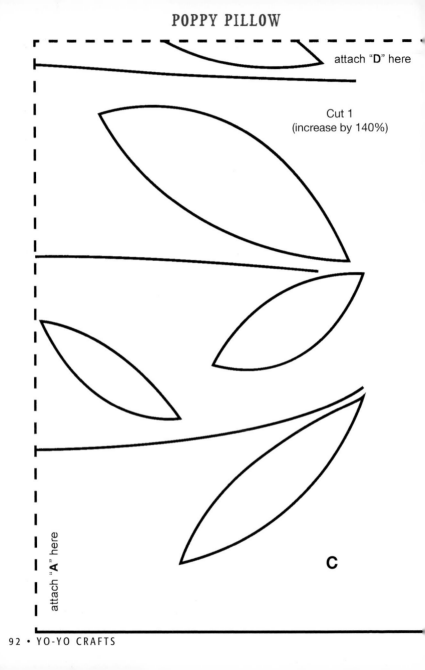

attach "**D**" here

Cut 1
(increase by 140%)

attach "**A**" here

C

POPPY PILLOW

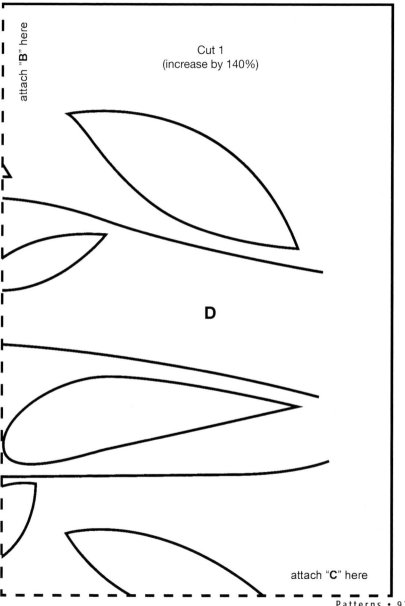

attach "**B**" here

Cut 1
(increase by 140%)

D

attach "**C**" here

This shows how the pattern will look when A, B, C, and D are assembled.

ICING DOTS TEMPLATE

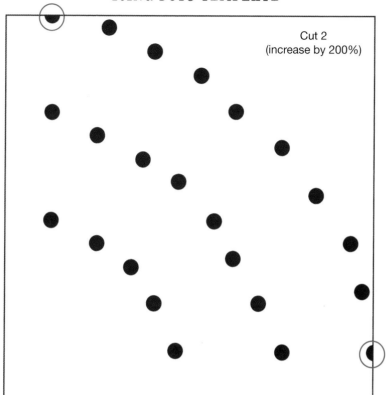

Cut 2
(increase by 200%)

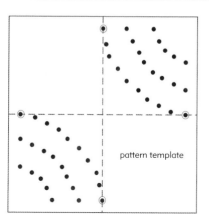

pattern template

Enlarge the Icing Dots template (above) by 200% so it measure 8-inches square. Make two copies and cut them out. Cut a piece of paper 16½ inches square. Mark a line all the way around ¼ inch from the edge, which will be the seam allowance. Place the two copies of the icing dots template on opposite sides of the pattern template as shown at left, lining up the outside corners on the drawn lines. Use a lightbox or tape to a window to transfer the dot locations to the fabric. NOTE: Yo-yos circled in red are not cut off the pattern but straddle the intersection lines. Place these 4 the same way as the others.

About the Authors

Jodie Davis is best known as the author of 30 quilting books. She also produces and hosts on QNNtv.com — the online television station devoted to all things quilting — two monthly series, *Quilt Out Loud* and *Quilt It!* Jayne Davis has been crafting for years, and she and co-author Jodie Davis are the authors of several craft books. As Jodie and Jayne discovered, creating alone is fun, but creating together is a blast. Whether scouring antiques stores for just the right find, fondling yard goods in a fabric store, or flipping through magazines, they have found that two heads are way better than one when it comes to designing — and having a great time while doing so.